SUPERHERO THEMES

T0087044

ISBN 978-1-5400-9491-9

Visit Hal Leonard Online at
www.halleonard.com

Contact us:
Hal Leonard
7777 West Bluemound Road
Milwaukee, WI 53213
ail: info@halleonard.com

In Europe, contact:
Hal Leonard Europe Limited
42 Wigmore Street
Marylebone, London, W1U 2RN
Email: info@halleonardeurope.com

In Australia, contact:
Hal Leonard Australia Pty. Ltd.
4 Lentara Court
Cheltenham, Victoria, 3192 Australia
ail: info@halleonard.com.au

THEME FROM ANT-MAN

from MARVEL'S ANT-MAN

Music by CHRISTOPHE BECK

Moderately fast

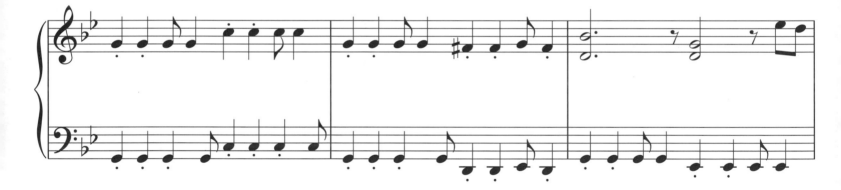

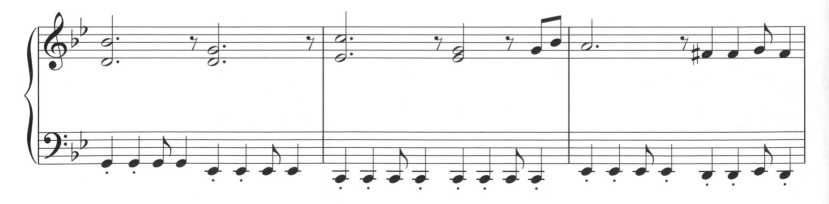

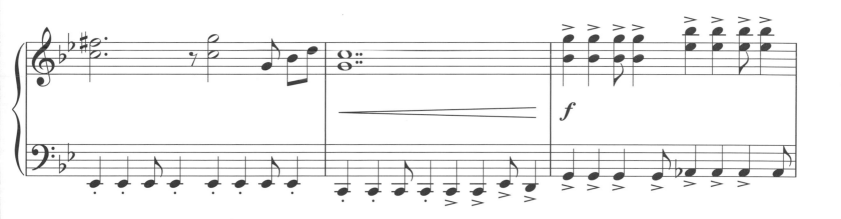

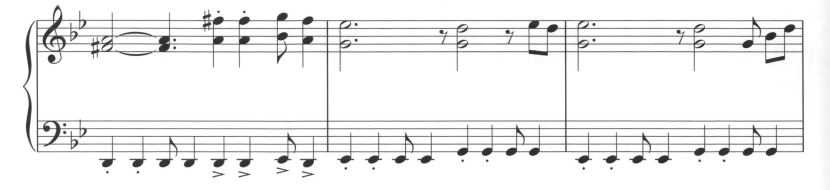

AVENGERS UNITE

from AVENGERS: AGE OF ULTRON

Music by DANNY ELFMAN

Moderately fast

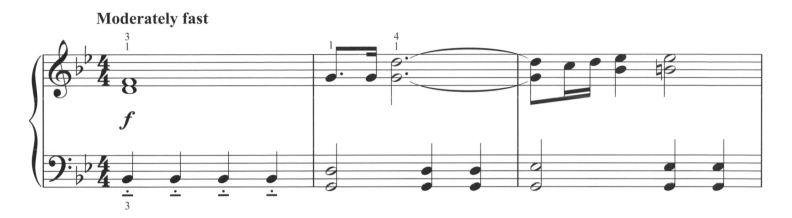

6

BATMAN THEME

Words and Music by
NEAL HEFTI

Bat Rock tempo

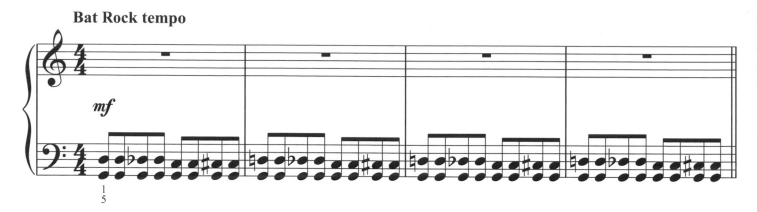

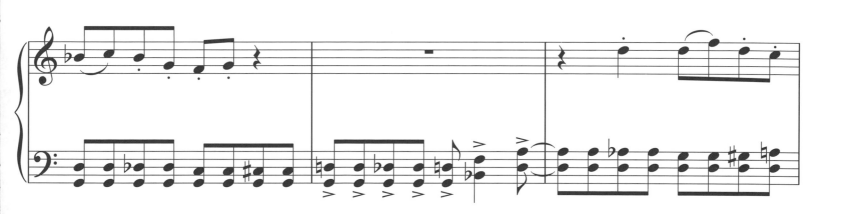

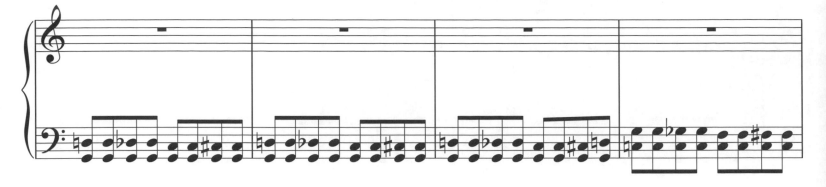

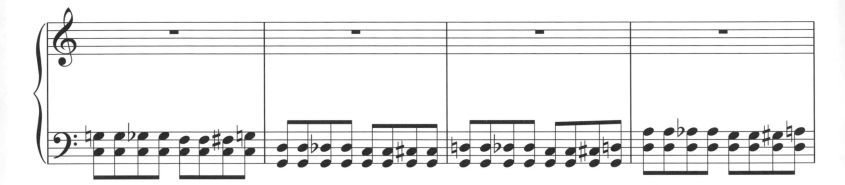

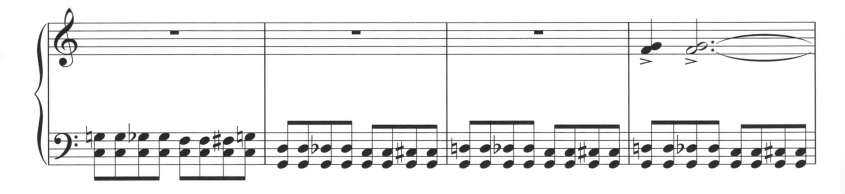

CAPTAIN AMERICA MARCH

from CAPTAIN AMERICA

By ALAN SILVESTRI

March tempo

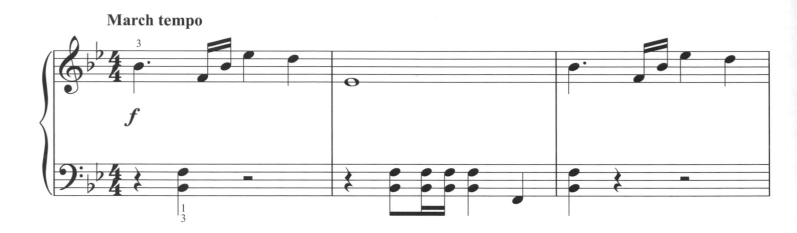

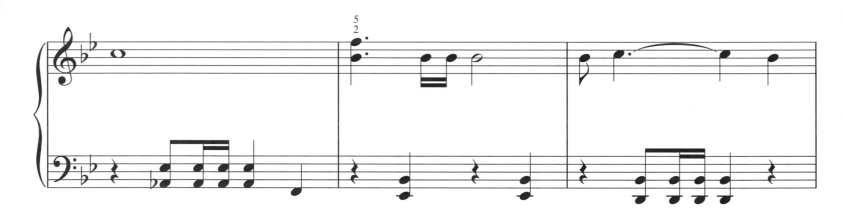

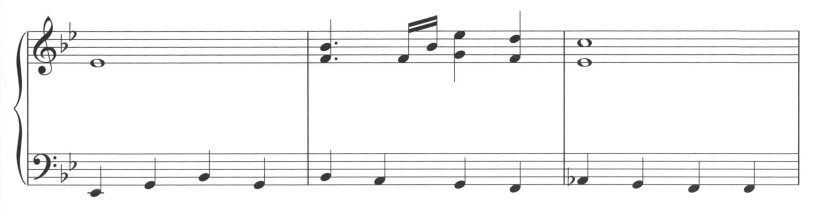

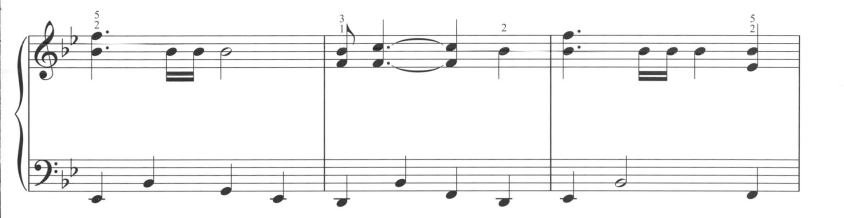

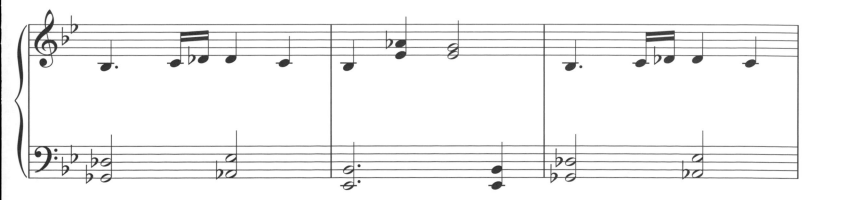

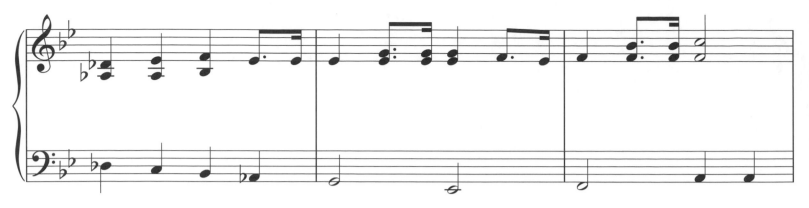

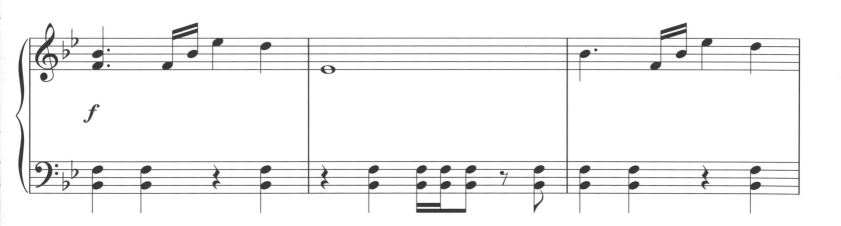

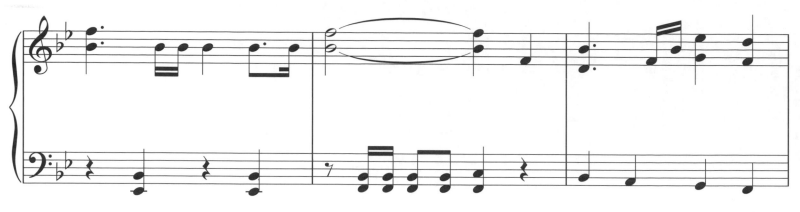

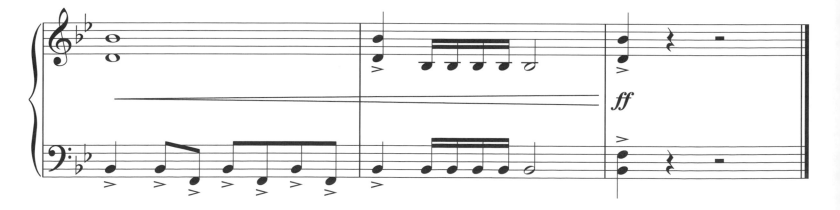

GUARDIANS INFERNO
from GUARDIANS OF THE GALAXY VOL. 2

Words and Music by JAMES GUNN
and TYLER BATES

Majestic

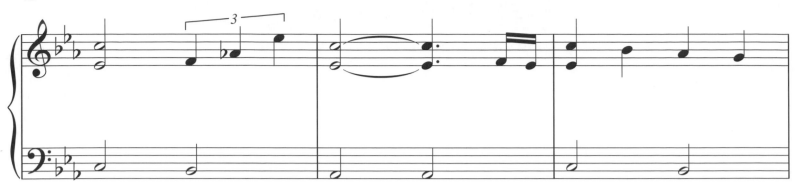

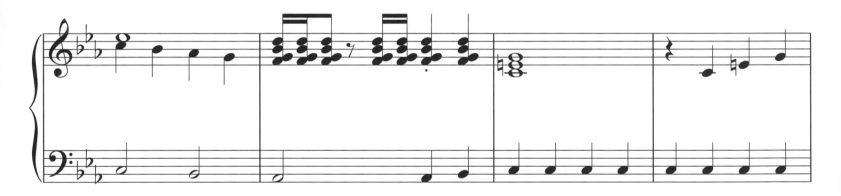

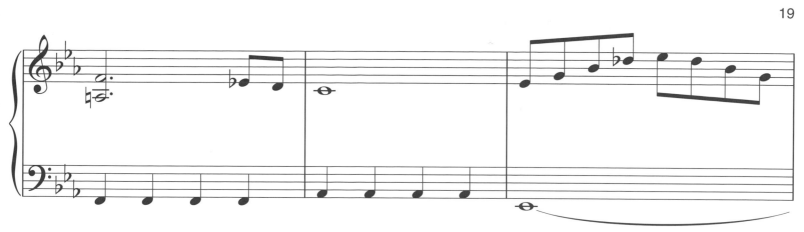

Solemn

ELASTIGIRL IS BACK

from INCREDIBLES 2

Composed by MICHAEL GIACCHINO

Moderately fast

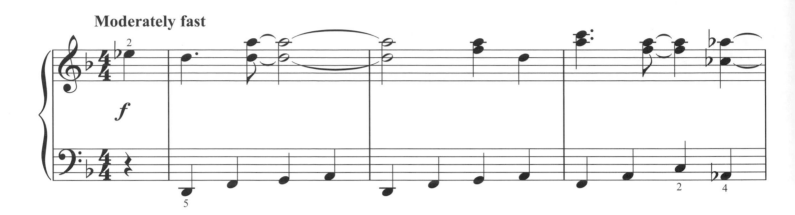

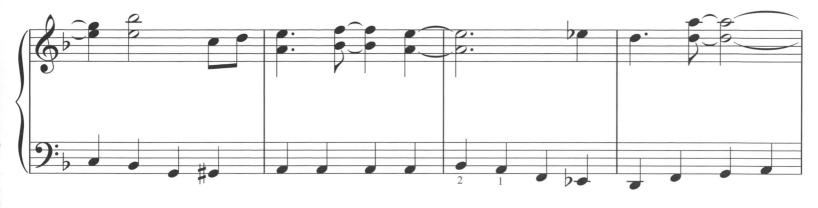

IMMORTALS
from BIG HERO 6

Words and Music by ANDREW HURLEY,
JOE TROHMAN, PATRICK STUMP
and PETE WENTZ

Moderate Rock

They say we are what we are,
Some-times the on-ly pay-off

but we don't have to be.
for hav-ing an-y faith

I'm bad be-hav-ior, but I
is when it's test-ed a-gain

do it in the best way.
and a-gain ev-'ry day.

I'll be the watch-er, watch-er
I'm still com-par-ing your past

of the e-ter-nal flame,
to my fu-ture.

I'll be the guard dog
It might be your wound

of all your fe-ver dreams.)
but they're my su-tures.

Oh, I am the

sand in the bot-tom half of the | hour - glass, glass, glass. | Oh, _____

_____ I'll try to | pic-ture me with-out you but I | can't. 'Cause we could be im-

or - tals, i - i - i - i-im - mor - tals. Just | not for long, _ for

long. And live with me for - ev - er | now, you pull the black-out cur-tains | down. _ Just

24

2.

I - i - i - i - i-im-mor - tals.   And live with me for-ev - er

now, _ now, _ now, _ now, _   pull the black-out cur-tains   down, _ down, _ down, _ down. _

We could be im - mor - tals,   i - i - i - i-im -

D.S. al Coda

CODA

mor - tals.   Just

i - i - i - i - i-im-mor - tals.
rit.

THE INCREDITS
from THE INCREDIBLES

Music by
MICHAEL GIACCHINO

Fast

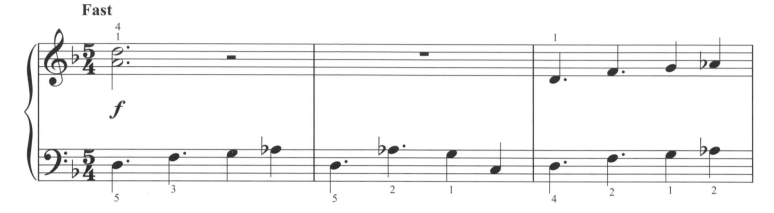

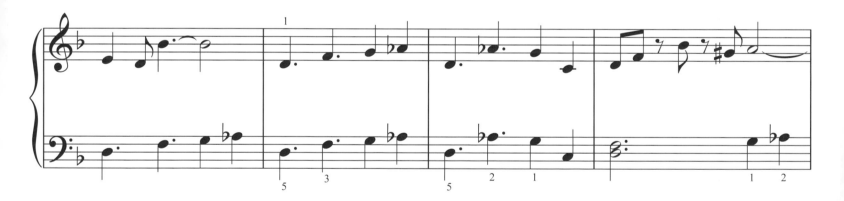

Play 3 times

IRON MAN
from IRON MAN

By RAMIN DJAWADI

Moderately

Faster

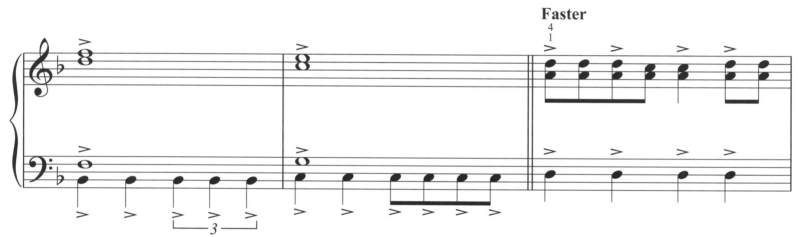

ROCKETEER END TITLES
from THE ROCKETEER

By JAMES HORNER

Slowly

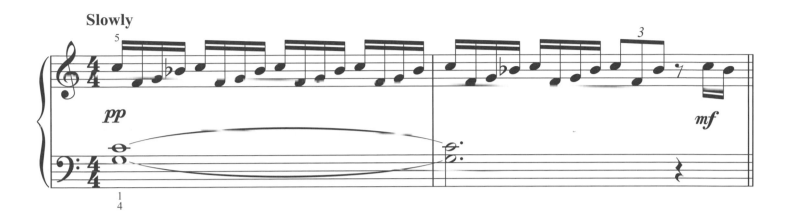

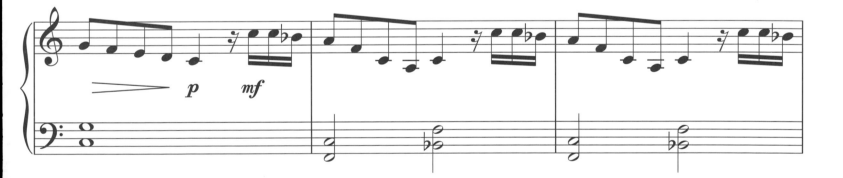

Slightly faster

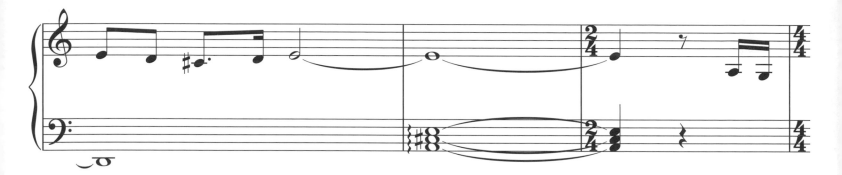

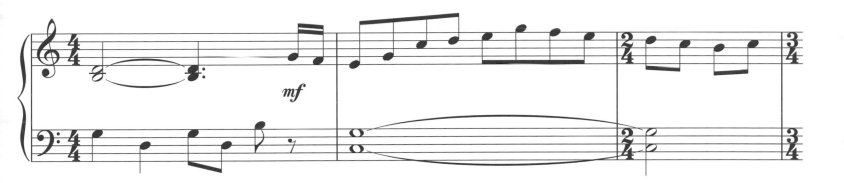

POW! POW! POW!
MR. INCREDIBLE'S THEME

from INCREDIBLES 2

Music and Lyrics by
MICHAEL GIACCHINO

Moderately fast

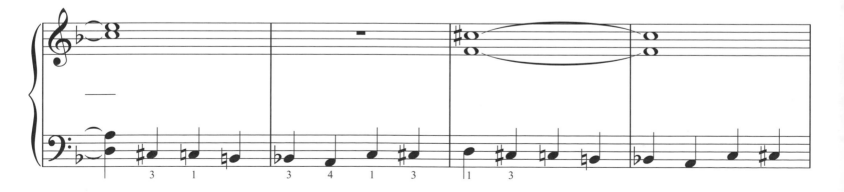

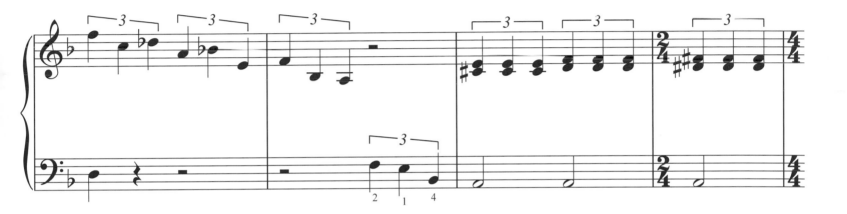

Mis - ter In - cred - i - ble, ___ In - cred - i - ble, ___ In - cred - i - ble, ___

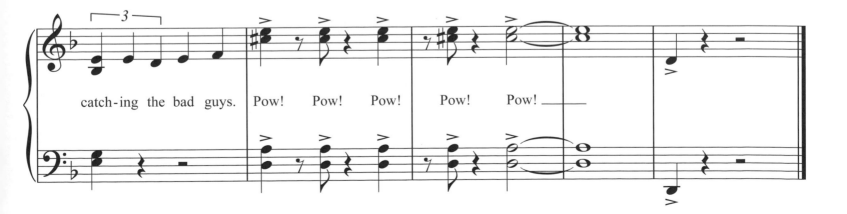

catch-ing the bad guys. Pow! Pow! Pow! Pow! Pow! ___

WAKANDA
from BLACK PANTHER

Music by LUDWIG GÖRANSSON

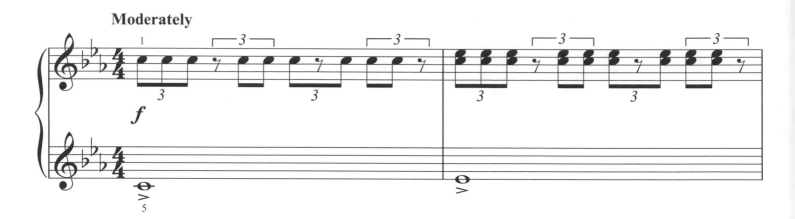

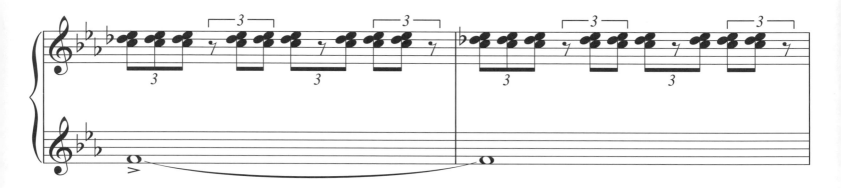

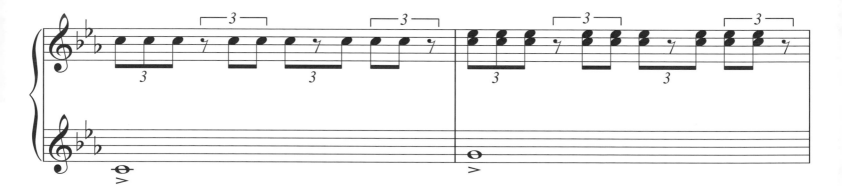

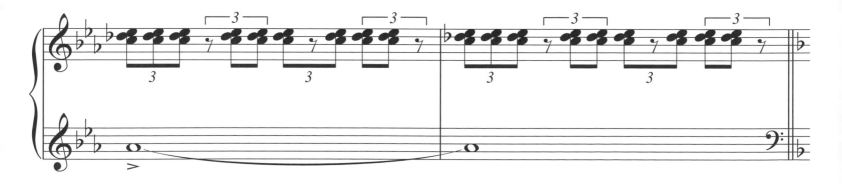

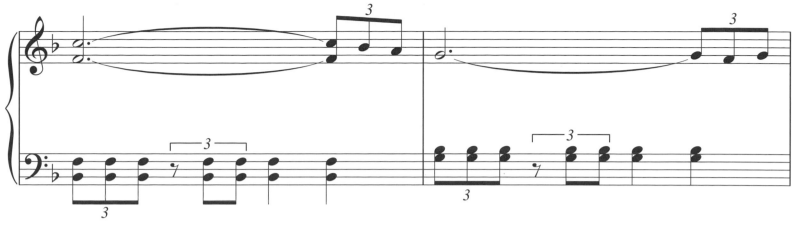

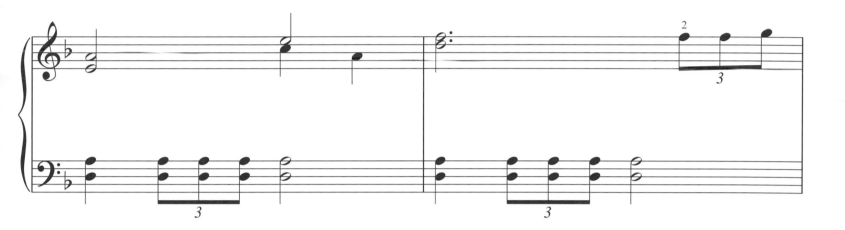

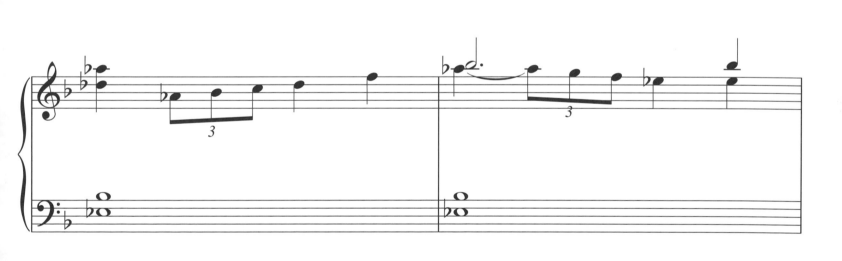

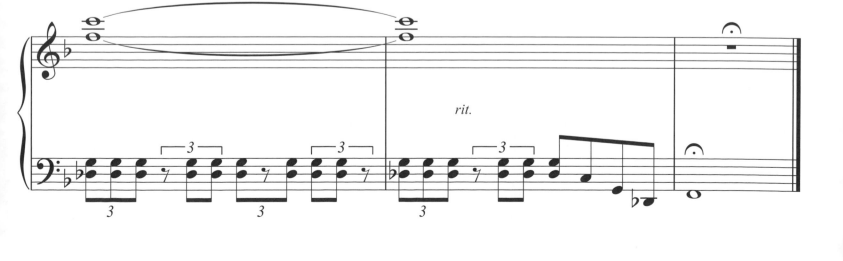

X-MEN APOCALYPSE - END TITLES

from X-MEN: APOCALYPSE

By JOHN OTTMAN

Moderately, with intensity

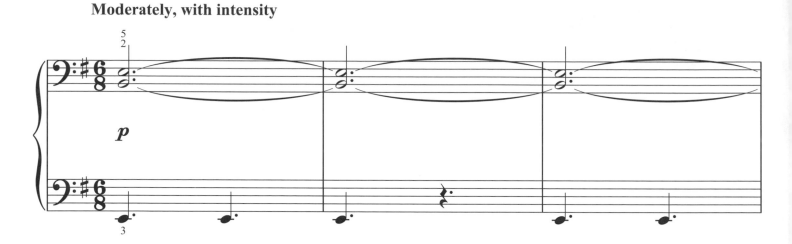

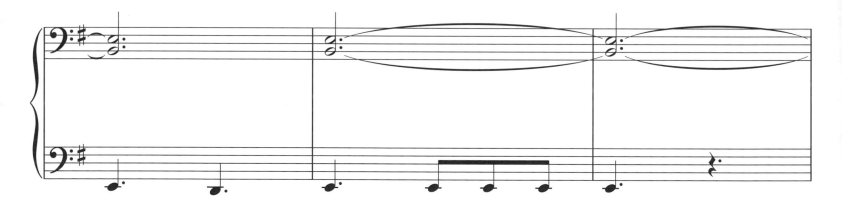

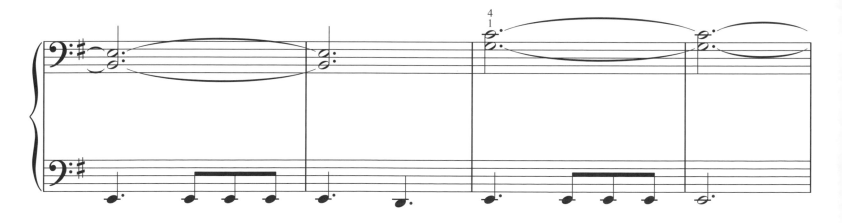

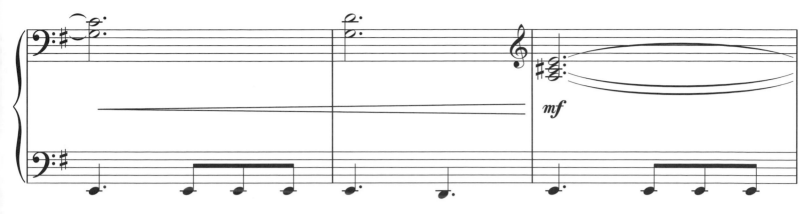

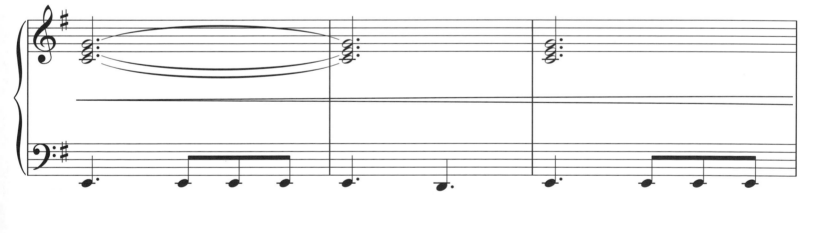

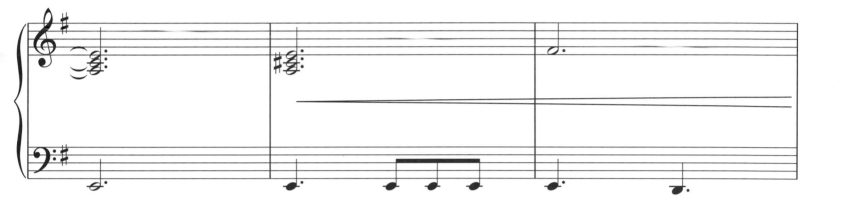

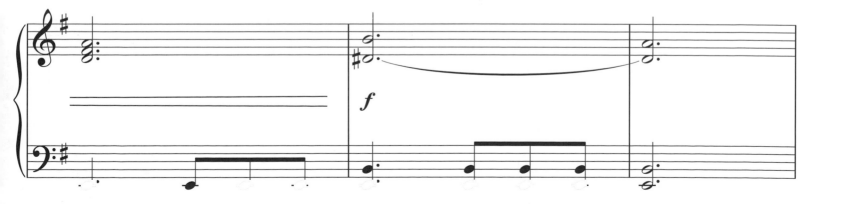

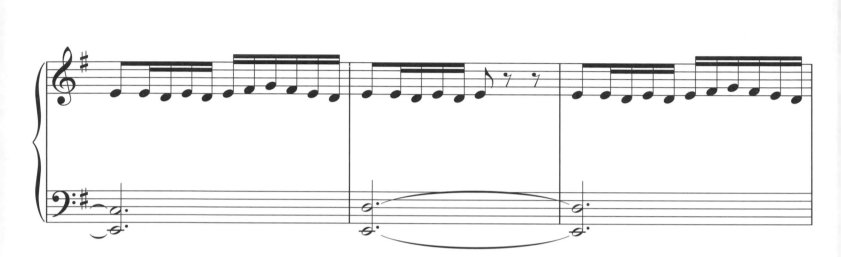

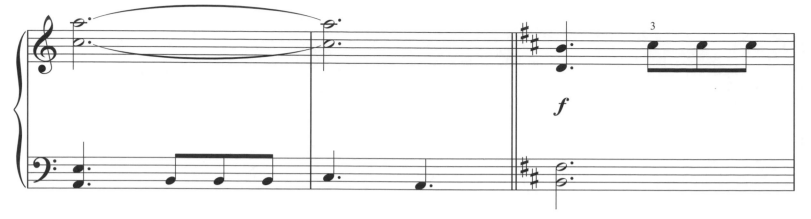

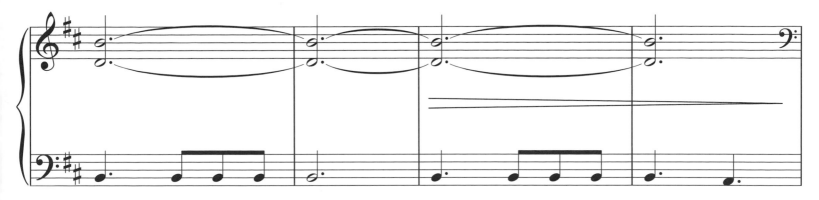

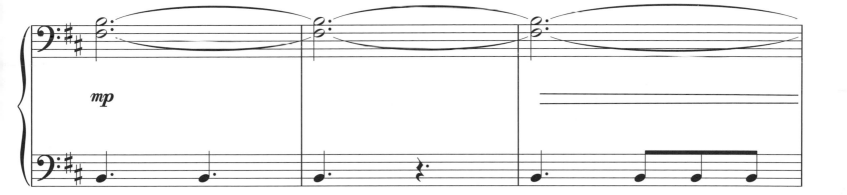

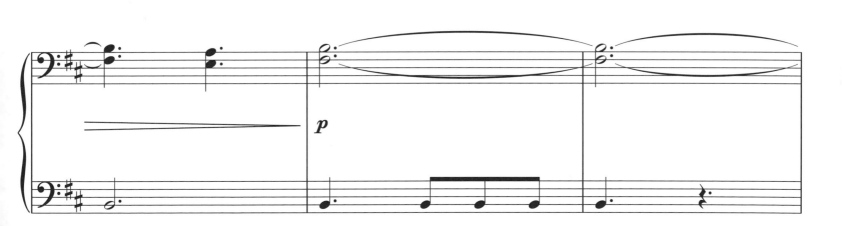

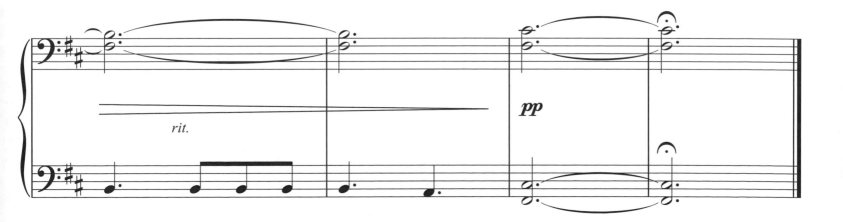

THEME FROM SPIDER MAN

Written by BOB HARRIS
and PAUL FRANCIS WEBSTER

Fast

Spi - der Man, ___ Spi - der Man, ___ does what - ev - er a
Is he strong? Lis - ten, bud; ___ he's got ra - di - o -

spi - der can. ___ Spins a web ___ an - y size, ___
ac - tive blood. __ Can he swing ___ from a thread? ___

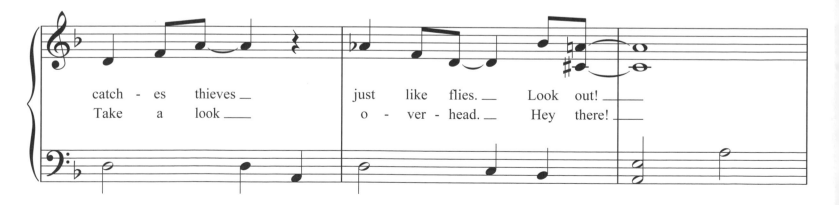

catch - es thieves ___ just like flies. ___ Look out! ___
Take a look ___ o - ver - head. ___ Hey there! ___

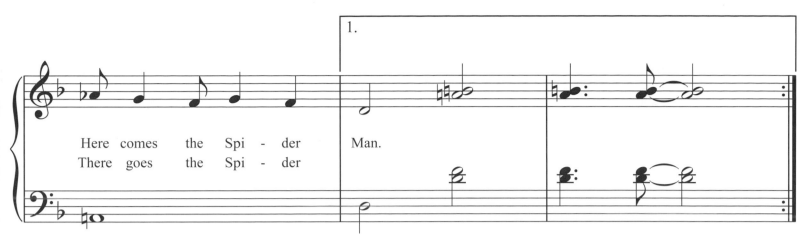

1.

Here comes the Spi - der Man.
There goes the Spi - der

2.

Man. *mp* In the chill of night, ___ at the

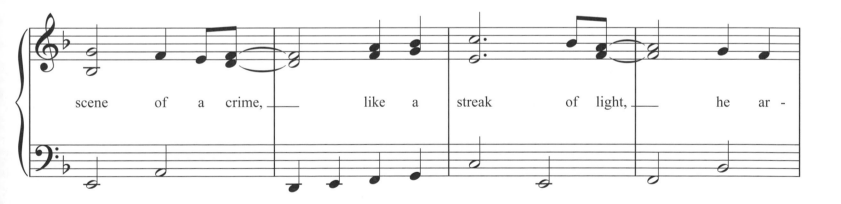

scene of a crime, ___ like a streak of light, ___ he ar -

rives just in time! ___ Spi - der Man, ___ *f*

48

Spi - der Man, __ friend - ly neigh - bor-hood Spi - der Man. __

Wealth and fame __ he's ig - nored. __ Ac - tion is ____

his re - ward. __ To him, __ life is a great big bang up. __

When - ev - er there's a hang up, ____ you'll find the Spi - der Man.